Contents

- 2 Unstressed vowels
- 3 Spelling clues
- 4 Connectives
- 5 Our changing language
- 6 Conventional English
- 7 Active and passive verbs
- 8 Clauses in complex sentences
- 9 Brackets
- 10 Personification
- 11 Biography and autobiography
- 12 Proverbs
- 13 Adverbs
- 14 Spelling rules
- 15 Connectives in complex sentences
- 16 Contracting sentences
- 17 Conditionals
- 18 Constructing arguments
- 19 Inventing words
- 20 Word games
- 21 Formal writing
- 22 Play scripts
- 23 Prepositions
- 24 Mnemonics
- 25 Using dictionaries
- 26 Direct and reported speech
- 27 More spelling rules
- 28 Similes
- 29 Rhyme and assonance
- 30 Narrator
- 31 Another spelling rule
- 32 Answers

AGES 10–11
KEY STAGE 2

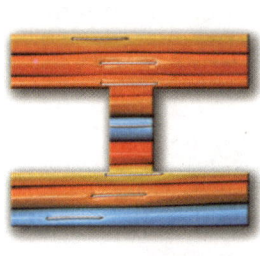

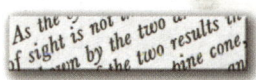

Premier ENGLISH

Unstressed vowels

Some words contain vowels that are difficult to hear when you say the word out loud.

general

frightening

In lots of these words, the unstressed vowel is e, followed by r or n.

I Underline the unstressed e in each word, then look at the letter which follows it to help you decide whether the word belongs in the er or en column.

a interest
b desperate
c generally
d widening
e generous
f deafening
g offering
h literature

er	en

II Sort these words into groups depending on the unstressed vowel each contains.

a stationary
b factory
c jewellery
d stationery
e reference
f category
g conference
h boundary
i difference
j lottery
k history
l voluntary

ary

ory

ery

erence

Spelling clues

Shared word roots, prefixes and suffixes can help us to spell whole groups of words.

tele means 'far off'

television   telephone   teleport

I Sort these words into groups with common prefixes.

reply	preview	audible	prime	transport	primate
transplant	primary	reconsider	prevent	audience
repeat	transfer	audition	prehistoric

audi = hear

trans = across

re = again

prim = first

pre = before

II Choose a suffix in bold from the box to complete these word sums.

scope = look   **clude** = shut   **port** = carry

a peri   + _____ = _____

b se   + _____ = _____

c trans + _____ = _____

d tele   + _____ = _____

e in   + _____ = _____

f micro + _____ = _____

g im   + _____ = _____

h con   + _____ = _____

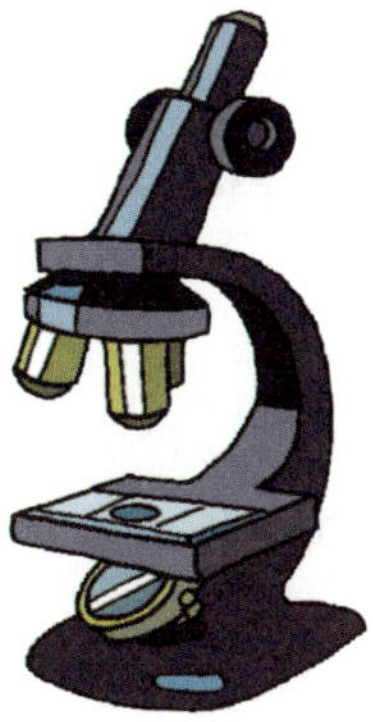

Connectives

Connectives are words or phrases used to extend sentences or join two sentences together.

Some are single words.

We ran fast **so** we wouldn't be late.

Some are compound words.

We visit our friends **whenever** we have time.

Some are phrases.

We played hockey **in spite of** the rain.

Pick a word from the box to complete each compound connective. Then write the whole word at the end.

| standing   over   ever   while   more   as   forward   less |

a when + _____   = _____

b mean + _____   = _____

c more + _____   = _____

d where + _____   = _____

e further + _____   = _____

f none + the + _____   = _____

g not + with + _____   = _____

h hence + _____   = _____

Draw lines to match up the pairs of connective words and phrases with similar meanings.

a in addition to   as a result
b in spite of   at the same time
c consequently   another thing
d meanwhile   as well as
e henceforth   in order that
f whenever   despite
g so that   every time
h furthermore   from now on

4

Our changing language

Words and expressions change over time.

Some words and phrases have been replaced by more modern ones.

whenas   has become   **whenever**

 Draw lines to match up these old-fashioned words with their modern meanings.

a tarry   look at
b hark   here
c behold   there
d verily   listen to
e yonder   from where
f whence   stay
g hither   you
h thee   truly

 Write down the modern meanings of these old-fashioned words.

a nigh _____
b foe _____
c beauteous _____
d saith _____
e ye _____
f whereto _____
g prithee _____
h begone _____

Conventional English

All sentences contain a noun or pronoun, and a verb.

If the noun or pronoun is singular, you must use the singular verb form.

If the noun or pronoun is plural, you must use the plural verb form.

The girl **runs** home.

The boys **play** football.

I Complete the chart by filling in the missing singular and plural verbs.

	singular nouns			plural nouns	
a	I	run	They	_____
b	She	tries	We	_____
c	The man	sings	The men	_____
d	The girl	swims	The girls	_____
e	The bird	_____	The birds	fly
f	He	_____	They	wash
g	The boy	_____	The boys	sleep
h	The child	_____	The children	play

II Circle the correct noun in bold to complete each sentence.

a The **teacher   teachers**   marks the books.
b The **cat   cats**   chase the mouse.
c The **boy   boys**   reads the book.
d The **horses   horse**   eat the grass.
e My **brother   brothers**   plays football.
f The **girls   girl**   walk home from school.
g The **train   trains**   were late.
h The **shop   shops**   was shut.

6

Active and passive verbs

Verbs can be active or passive.

John **ate** the cake.

This verb is **active**.
It describes John's action.

The cake **was eaten** by John.

This verb is **passive**. It describes what happens to the cake.

Passive sentences often sound clumsy, unless some of the information is missed out of the sentence.

The window **was broken**.

This sentence creates suspense, because we don't know how the window was broken.

I Tick the box that correctly describes each sentence.

active   passive

a The wind blew my hat off.
b I lost the key on the way home.
c Our house was broken into.
d The letter was written by Max.
e Dad drove us to school.
f My hair was trimmed by the barber.
g Millie kicked the ball.
h Arjan broke the window.
i The garden was covered by the snow.
j The candle was blown out by the draught.

II Write these passive sentences again, using active verbs.

a The mouse was chased by the cat. _____
b My clothes were soaked by the rain. _____
c The missing book was found by Sam. _____
d The door was opened by Jo. _____
e My magazine was delivered by the paperboy. _____
f Our test papers were marked by the teacher. _____

Clauses in complex sentences

A clause is a group of words that describe an event or situation.

Complex sentences contain more than one clause. They often contain a **main clause** and a **subordinate clause**.

The **main clause** makes sense on its own. The **subordinate clause** adds extra information, but would not make sense on its own.

It was cold so I wore a coat.
main clause — subordinate clause

I Underline the main clause in these sentences.

a Who is that, knocking at the door?
b I felt ill, so I went to bed.
c We went swimming in the river.
d It was dark when we got home.
e We went to Italy for our holiday.
f I broke the vase when I was dusting.
g Mum made me a cake for my birthday.
h The car broke down, because it had run out of petrol.
i Gran went shopping to buy some slippers.
j I drew a picture to hang on the wall.

II Write a suitable subordinate clause to complete these complex sentences.

a I tidied my room so that _____.
b We went shopping for _____.
c The dog barked, because _____.
d It was a hot day, so _____.
e I picked some flowers _____.
f We posted the letter to _____.
g They kept running until _____.
h I lost my bag when _____.
i The bus was full, so _____.
j I peeled the potatoes _____.

8

Brackets

We can use brackets to add extra useful information to a sentence. Brackets don't disrupt the meaning of the sentence, so you can take them out of a sentence without changing its meaning.

The monster's bad breath **(and smelly feet)** meant he had no friends.

I Choose a sensible phrase from the box to complete each sentence.

| but before tea | kicked by Paul | and freezing wind |
| which he cut himself | a ham sandwich | a tabby |

a The cat (_____) curled up and went to sleep.

b The packed lunch (_____) was delicious.

c After school (_____) we played in the park.

d The cold rain (_____) kept us indoors.

e My little brother's hair (_____) looks dreadful.

f The football (_____) flew over the fence.

II Rewrite these sentences, adding the brackets in a sensible place.

a My best friend is called Lily. (who is ten)
_____

b The old dog was dirty. (and smelly)
_____

c Pink is my favourite colour. (but not pale pink)
_____

d My new coat is really warm. (bought yesterday)
_____

e My new school is really big. (where I'm going in September)
_____

f The school holiday is going to be great. (which starts next week)
_____

Personification

Personification is where a writer describes something using words we would normally use to describe a person.

The wind **sighed** in the trees.

Love is **blind**.

 Underline the personification in this passage of writing.

We sat by the ruined cottage to have our picnic. The sun smiled down on us, and birds chattered in the trees. All around us, buttercups danced in the breeze, and the nodding branches of a willow tree sheltered us from the fierce sun. The broken windows of the deserted cottage stared silently towards the sleeping hills in the distance, and the wind whispered secrets through the empty rooms.

 Use personification to write descriptions of these things.

a a stream trickling over stones
_____

b an owl hooting
_____

c a rusty gate squeaking
_____

d storm clouds gathering
_____

e stars twinkling
_____

f bees humming
_____

Biography and autobiography

It can be very interesting to read about the lives of famous or interesting people.

An **autobiography** is the life story of a person, written by that person. Autobiographies tend to be written in the first person.

> I was born in Dublin in 1908.

A **biography** is also a life story, but it is written by somebody else. Biographies are written in the third person.

> She was born in Dublin in 1908.

I Tick whether each sentence comes from a biography or an autobiography.

		biography	autobiography
a	He was a fair and popular king, who brought peace and prosperity to his subjects.	☐	☐
b	I left school at the age of 14 and went to work in a milliner's shop.	☐	☐
c	My father was in the army so we moved around a lot.	☐	☐
d	Her acting career began at the age of seven, when she appeared in a TV commercial.	☐	☐
e	We lived in a street of small, terraced houses, each with a small back yard.	☐	☐
f	She worked tirelessly to develop the vaccine.	☐	☐

II This is a short extract from the autobiography of a fictional sportswoman. Rewrite it as a biography.

> When I was eight, I was sent to a strict girls' boarding school. I missed my family terribly and never settled into school life, so I was thrilled when the war came and I was evacuated to Wales with my three brothers. For the next four years we lived on a farm, so it was a dreadful shock to return to post-war London, and to school.

_____
_____
_____
_____
_____
_____
_____

Proverbs

Proverbs are **wise sayings**. They are often very old, but most of them are still true!

Too many cooks spoil the broth.

I **Complete these proverbs.**

a The grass is always greener _____.

b The early bird _____.

c A bird in the hand is worth _____.

d Great minds _____.

e Every cloud _____.

f A bad workman _____.

g Many a true word is _____.

h Let sleeping dogs _____.

II **Write down what you think each of these proverbs means.**

a Many hands make light work.
_____

b Don't put all your eggs in one basket.
_____

c Two heads are better than one.
_____

d A stitch in time saves nine.
_____

e Out of the frying pan, into the fire.
_____

f Don't count your chickens before they hatch.
_____

g Look before you leap.
_____

Adverbs

Adverbs **describe verbs**. They can tell us the following things:

How – for example, slowly, quickly

When – for example, now, soon, later

Where – for example, here, outside

How often – for example, rarely, never

 Circle the adverb in each sentence.

a   Jamie slipped silently out of the door.

b   Jo ran outside.

c   We ate quickly so we could go and play.

d   You never do your homework.

e   We'll make it later.

f   Dad left the shopping there.

g   The tortoise crawled slowly down the garden.

h   Mum shouted angrily.

i   Sam skated unsteadily on the slippery floor.

j   I always save my pocket money.

 Pick a sensible adverb from the box to complete each sentence.

| soon | nearly | here | soundly | quickly | happily | always | brightly |

a   Joshua sprinted _____ home.

b   Bring the book _____.

c   The stars twinkled _____ in the sky.

d   We _____ have fish and chips on Friday.

e   I've _____ finished my book.

f   The little girl smiled _____.

g   The baby slept _____.

h   My friend will be here _____.

13

Spelling rules

Learning spelling rules can help us to spell whole families of words.

Using a spelling rule can help us to add a suffix to words that end in a consonant then y.

You can usually add the suffixes ing, and ly, without changing the spelling of the base word.

With ness, er, est, ed, and sometimes ly, you need to change the final y of the base word to **i** before you add the suffix.

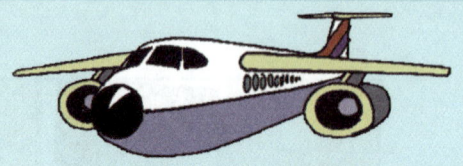

fly + ing = flying

greedy + ness = greediness

I Complete these word sums using the rules above.

a empty + ness = _____
b fry + ing = _____
c deny + ed = _____
d ready + ly = _____
e sleepy + ly = _____
f windy + er = _____
g silly + ness = _____
h carry + ing = _____
i friend + ly = _____

II Choose the correct spelling from the words in bold to complete each sentence.

a The cat stretched _____. **lazyly   lazily**

b The lion looked _____ at us. **hungrily   hungryly**

c We _____ to find the way home. **tried   tryed**

d I _____ to the question the teacher asked. **replied   replyed**

e The prince _____ the princess. **marryed   married**

f Kate was bursting with _____ when she saw her present. **happiness   happyness**

g Dad carried the _____ bag. **heavyest   heaviest**

h My kitten is _____ than all the others. **prettier   prettyer**

i He was _____ of the spider. **terrifyed   terrified**

Connectives in complex sentences

A complex sentence has more than one clause. Connective words and phrases can be used to join these two clauses together.

It was my birthday, **so** I had a party.

first clause   second clause

I **Underline the connective word or phrase in each of these complex sentences.**

a I did my homework while Dad cooked tea.

b Sally wore her coat, because it was cold.

c We were late, so we had to run.

d Marc got into trouble, because of his untidy bedroom.

e I love tennis, but netball is better.

f I enjoyed the film, although I had seen it before.

g We had our breakfast before we went to school.

h Eva saved her pocket money, so she could buy the CD.

II **Write each pair of simple sentences again as one complex sentence, joined by a connective from the box.**

| although | so | while | before | but | because |

a I had a lie in. It was Saturday.
_____

b It was hot. We bought some ice creams.
_____

c Max counted to twenty. His friends hid.
_____

d We packed our suitcase. We left for the airport.
_____

e Susie won second prize. Alice won first prize.
_____

f John drank his tea quickly. It was hot.
_____

15

Contracting sentences

Sometimes, we can take the really important information from a piece of writing, then write it again in a form we can use more quickly.

If we make **notes**, we just write down key words that will jog our memory later. Notes don't have to be complete sentences.

If we write a **summary**, we rewrite the most important information in complete sentences.

I **Underline the key words in this piece of writing.**

The Vikings invaded Britain more than a thousand years ago. They sailed from Sweden, Norway and Denmark in longboats, and raided the coasts and rivers of the United Kingdom. Many also settled here and farmed the land. Viking families lived in houses made from wood, stone or turf, with a hole in the roof to let out the smoke from the cooking fires. They believed in many gods, but the most popular were Odin, the wise and one-eyed, and Thor, the god of thunder.

II **Now write a set of notes, and a summary, of the piece of writing using the words you have just underlined to help you.**

Notes:

_____
_____
_____
_____
_____
_____
_____

Summary:

_____
_____
_____
_____
_____
_____
_____

fancy + full =	wolf + s =	hero + s =
pity + full =	mouse + s =	echo + s =
thief + s =	lorry + s =	disco + s =

thieves	lorries	discos
pitiful	mice	echoes
fanciful	wolves	heroes

varied	laziness	digger
married	shameless	hugging
heavier	wettest	helped

vary + ed =	lazy + ness =	dig + er =
marry + ed =	shame + less =	hug + ing =
heavy + er =	wet + est =	help + ed =

Conditionals

We use conditionals to show that one thing happening depends on something else.

We'll go **if** there's time.

 Underline the conditionals in these sentences.

a If you use matches, you might burn yourself.

b Going to the fair would be brilliant.

c I can come to your party, if I finish my homework.

d If we're not greedy, we'll have enough sweets for all of us.

e Missing the bus might make us late for school.

f I'll feel better after I've had something to eat.

g When my bike is mended, I'm going for a ride.

h When I'm older, I can stay up late.

i When I go to bed, I'll read my book.

II **Use the conditionals in bold to help you write sensible endings for these sentences.**

a **If** it is raining _____.

b **Unless** you're too tired _____.

c **Should** I win the competition _____.

d **When** it is cold _____.

e Cheating in the test **might** _____.

f Helping Mum **should** _____.

g Going to bed early **might** _____.

h Having six kittens **would be** _____.

i I will get my allowance **if** I _____.

j **When** we get home _____.

Constructing arguments

When you are writing an argument, you will want to persuade your readers to agree with your point of view.

If you think about the objections your readers might have to your idea, you can include answers to them in your argument.

Although most children don't like doing homework, it does help them to practise what they have learnt at school.

You can also provide evidence to support your view.

A survey at our school found that children who do their homework are more likely to do well in their tests.

I Imagine you are going to write an argument in favour of wearing school uniform. Look at the pieces of fictional evidence below. Underline the ones that could help to support your argument.

a The cost of school uniform has risen by 40%.

b Reports show that schools with uniforms have less bullying because all the children are wearing the same.

c School clothing is specially designed to be durable and easy to care for.

d Research by clothing stores argues that fashion clothing lets children express their personalities.

e About 60% of children say they have less fashion clothing because their parents have to buy uniform as well.

f A survey of headteachers says that schools with uniforms have a higher profile in the local community.

g Motoring groups warn that the dark colour of most winter school uniforms makes it hard for children to be seen by motorists at night.

II Write down three objections your readers may have against wearing uniform and how you could answer them in your argument.

Your readers may argue	You could answer
a	
b	
c	

Inventing words

Most of the words we use can be found in the dictionary, but occasionally we can make up our own words, using prefixes and suffixes with set meanings.

micro + phobia = microphobia
small   fear   fear of small things

I Imagine you are writing a science fiction story based in the future. Lots of the things you need to write about haven't been invented yet, so there are no words for them. Look at the meanings of the suffixes and prefixes in the box. Then use them to help you invent words for these things.

scope = look	phobia = fear	hydro = water	port = carry	phile = love
micro = small	graph = write	bi = two	octo = eight	tele = far off
audi = hear	phone = sound	photo = light	auto = self	

a A device that allows you to look in eight different directions at once. _____

b A station for underwater travel. _____

c An instrument that allows you to write very small, to save space. _____

d A camera that takes two pictures of you at the same time. _____

e A fear of things far away. _____

f A machine that creates a written record of sounds. _____

g A way of transporting objects and people in a beam of light. _____

h A machine which allows the same sound to be played in two different places at the same time. _____

II Use the words in the box above to help you work out what these made up words might mean.

a octophone _____

b photophile _____

c microport _____

d audiophobe _____

e hydrophile _____

f autoscope _____

Word games

Playing words games can improve your spelling and help you to learn new words.

I Find these sporting words in the word search grid. When you have finished, rearrange the red letters to make the name of a popular team game.

- a hockey
- b netball
- c squash
- d swimming
- e athletics
- f football
- g tennis
- h cricket
- i badminton
- j rounders

s	p	e	t	e	n	n	i	s	h	n
n	a	h	m	u	z	m	j	n	v	o
t	r	o	u	n	d	e	r	s	k	t
s	b	c	s	w	e	v	e	q	a	n
w	c	k	l	y	f	b	l	u	w	i
i	n	e	t	b	a	l	l	a	n	m
m	d	y	f	k	t	r	i	s	x	d
m	y	s	c	i	t	e	l	h	t	a
i	p	x	s	r	x	a	h	i	g	b
n	g	u	c	r	i	c	k	e	t	j
g	f	o	o	t	b	a	l	l	d	b
w	c	p	t	z	o	y	c	q	d	q

The mystery sport is ____ ____ ____ ____ ____.

II Use the clues to help you unscramble each group of letters into two words.

- a tacbhalire — You'll find these in the dining room. — _table_ _chair_
- b kfnioferk — You eat with these. — _____ _____
- c appepalre — Both fruits that grow on trees. — _____ _____
- d mosotanrs — You'll see these in the night sky. — _____ _____
- e shboeoosts — You wear these on your feet. — _____ _____
- f bmaogoazkine — You might read these. — _____ _____
- g cchhaeleske — These things are very different! — _____ _____
- h sapltepper — You put these on your food. — _____ _____

Formal writing

The language we use when we speak to each other is informal.

Do you want to come to my party?

Official written language is much more formal.

Jay requests the pleasure of your company at her party.

I Draw lines to match up the formal language with the less formal version on the signs.

a Breakages must be purchased.

b Kindly refrain from walking on the grass.

c Children are not permitted on the premises.

d Parking is prohibited.

e Kindly complete your purchases as the store is closing.

f Please submit all outstanding monies due immediately.

g Trespassing is forbidden.

> Please don't walk on the grass
>
> NO PARKING
>
> PLEASE PAY FOR YOUR SHOPPING AS THE STORE IS CLOSING
>
> You mustn't be here without permission
>
> PLEASE HAND OVER ALL THE MONEY YOU OWE RIGHT NOW!
>
> CHILDREN ARE NOT ALLOWED IN HERE
>
> YOU MUST PAY FOR ANYTHING YOU BREAK.

II Use informal language to write down what these sentences mean.

a Patrons are politely requested to vacate the premises promptly at 6 o'clock.

_____

b Non-compliance with club rules will invalidate membership.

_____

c Drivers failing to adhere to stated speed restrictions will be liable to a fine.

_____

d Travellers must be able to present a valid ticket upon request.

_____

e The management accepts no responsibility for property lost or damaged.

_____

f Refunds will only be made for faulty or damaged goods.

_____

Play scripts

Plays tell a story just like a piece of narrative writing, but most plays don't have a narrator to move the story along.

What the characters say and do on stage tells the story. The script contains the characters' lines and stage directions to tell them what to do.

I Imagine you are writing a film or TV script based on the section of story below. Write a description of the footpath, plus stage directions for Andy and Calum.

Andy and Calum hurried along the footpath. The moon that had been shining so brightly before had disappeared behind a cloud. 'Hurry!' said Andy. 'Let's get out of here.'

'What was that?' hissed Calum, spinning round to look behind them.

Setting: _____

_____

_____

_____

Stage directions for Andy: _____

_____

Stage directions for Calum: _____

_____

II Write a section of play script based on the passage from the story. Include the next few lines, where we discover what or who is following the boys down the path.

Prepositions

Prepositions are words like **at**, **in** or **to**. They can describe position, direction or time.

We went out **at** lunchtime.

He sat **on** the sofa.

I Circle the preposition in these sentence.

a It rained during the night.
b The cat ran up the tree.
c We went to the cinema.
d I waited behind you in the queue.
e Chloe sat on the stool.
f Jack climbed over the fence.
g The missing pen was under my bed.
h We are visiting friends on Friday.

II Imagine you are watching a fallen leaf blowing in the wind. Write a short paragraph about its journey to the ground, using each of the prepositions in the box.

| down   through   up   under   across   between   onto   around |

_____
_____
_____
_____
_____
_____
_____
_____
_____

23

Mnemonics

Mnemonics are slogans or phrases we can use to help us remember how to spell tricky words.

Some focus on a particular part of a word we find difficult.

sep**a**rate

move **a**way

We can also make them up to help us remember whole words.

knight

king's **n**aughty **i**mps **g**o **h**ome **t**onight

I Choose the word from the box that you think each of these mnemonics could help you to remember.

| beauty | Wednesday | receipt | bought | fluoride | sweet | typical | receive |

a **T**iny **y**ellow **p**eople **i**ce **c**akes **a** **l**ot. _____

b **F**at **l**azy **u**ncles' **o**gres **r**ace **i**nside **d**emanding **e**ggs. _____

c **W**itches **e**at **d**ead **n**ettles **e**very **s**ingle **d**ay. _____

d **B**lue **o**tters **u**nder **g**reen **h**ats **t**rade. _____

e **B**onny **e**lves **a**wait **u**gly **t**rolls **y**odelling. _____

f **R**uby **e**arrings **c**an **e**ven **i**nterest **v**ain **e**lephants. _____

g **S**ugary **w**onderful **e**xciting **e**dible **t**reat. _____

h **R**ats **e**at **c**hocolate **e**ggs **i**n **p**rivate **t**unnels. _____

II Write mnemonics for these words.

a conscious _____

b ambitious _____

c jealous _____

d politician _____

e frightened _____

f astronaut _____

g fiery _____

h placate _____

Using dictionaries

Dictionaries can help us to find out more about the spelling and meaning of groups of words with the same prefix.

I Write down three words that begin with each of the prefixes below. Use a dictionary to look up the meanings, then use the definitions to help you work out what each prefix means.

a mis = _____

b ex = _____

c sub = _____

II The words that match the three definitions in each group below share the same prefix. Write down the three words. Use a dictionary to check the meanings.

a to stop something from happening _____

   to say what will happen in the future _____

   to get something ready _____

b to make again _____

   to put something back _____

   to mend _____

c not to agree _____

   to get rid of _____

   to vanish _____

25

Direct and reported speech

When we are writing, we often need to record what people say.

Direct speech quotes the actual words the person says. We put it between speech marks.

'Look at my new skates,' said Leo.

Reported speech reports what someone says, but doesn't use their exact words.

She said she would be late.

I Turn the speech bubbles into sentences with direct speech.

_____
_____
_____
_____

II Rewrite these pieces of direct speech, as reported speech.

a Kate said, 'Fancy going bowling?'
_____

b 'Where's my school bag?' asked Jake.
_____

c 'Please be back by 6 o'clock,' said Mum.
_____

d Jamie said, 'I'm going to the beach tomorrow!'
_____

e Sally asked, 'Will we get there in time?'
_____

f 'Happy birthday!' shouted the twins.
_____

More spelling rules

We can use spelling rules to help us spell words where i and e appear together.

Many words have ie.

> tie   quiet

c is usually followed by ei: i before e, except after c

> conceit   receive

Other words with ei tend to have a long 'a' sound.

> vein   weigh

 Choose the correctly spelt words from each set in bold to complete these sentences.

a I ate two _____ of cake. **peices   pieces**

b I kept the _____, so I could take the dress back if it didn't fit. **receipt   reciept**

c A spider has _____ legs. **ieght   eight**

d Indira is my best _____. **friend   freind**

e My Dad loves apple _____. **pie   pei**

f Water was pouring through the _____. **ceiling   cieling**

g The bride wore a long white _____. **viel   veil**

h The _____ stole my bike. **thief   theif**

i We borrowed some eggs from our _____. **nieghbour   neighbour**

j On holiday, we visited a _____ castle. **medieval   medeival**

Underline the misspelt words in this piece of writing. Watch out for exceptions to the rules!

I love going to the museum. They have an anceint sheild that belonged to a brave knight during the riegn of a famous medeival king. They also have his sword, which is sharp enough to peirce armour. There's a modern copy too, so you can feel the wieght of it.

Also in the museum is a model of an Iron Age tribal cheif, and information about the beleifs his people held. You can watch a reconstruction of one of their battles, with feirce warriors racing across a feild shreiking. It really changed my veiw of history.

27

Similes

Similes create a picture in your reader's mind by comparing one thing to another, using the word **as** or **like**.

as weak **as** a lamb

sleeping **like** a baby

I Pick a noun from the box to complete these well-known similes.

chimney   bee   log   wind   fish   lark   hills   ox   bat   mouse

a as old as the _____
b as quiet as a _____
c as strong as an _____
d as blind as a _____
e as busy as a _____
f smoking like a _____
g run like the _____
h sing like a _____
i swims like a _____
j sleeping like a _____

II Think of ways to complete these similes.

a as _____ as a bear
b as bright as a _____
c as _____ as ice
d as young as _____
e eating like a _____
f jumping like _____
g _____ like thunder
h _____ like a horse

Rhyme and assonance

Rhyme and assonance can both be very effective in poetry and stories.

Assonance is where two or more words contain the same vowel sound. The words may also rhyme, but they don't have to.

sly   crime   resign

Rhyming words end with the same sound. Groups of rhyming words are also examples of assonance, because they contain the same vowel sound.

tongue   hung   young

I The groups of words below are all examples of assonance. Underline the groups that **don't** rhyme.

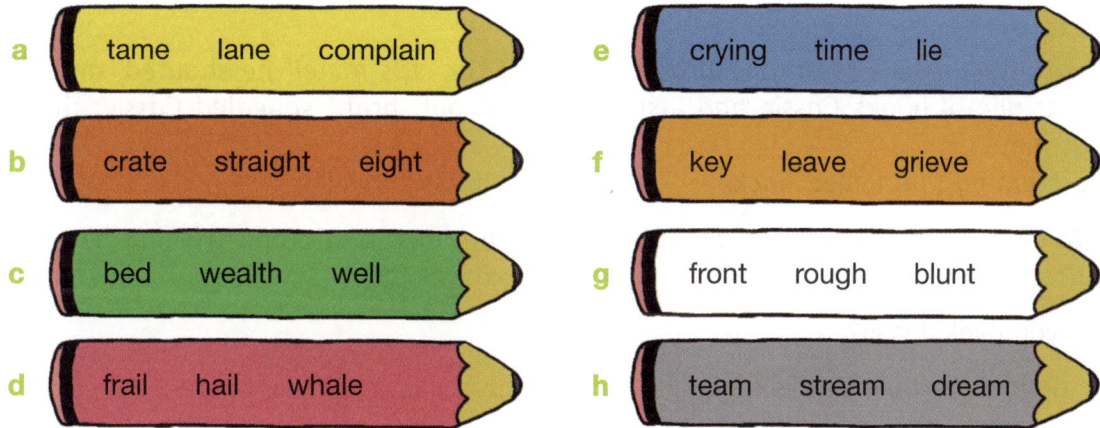

a tame   lane   complain
b crate   straight   eight
c bed   wealth   well
d frail   hail   whale
e crying   time   lie
f key   leave   grieve
g front   rough   blunt
h team   stream   dream

II For each of the words below, write down one example of rhyme and one of assonance. The first has been done for you.

		rhyme	assonance
a	clean	mean	perceive
b	out		
c	home		
d	child		
e	train		
f	buy		
g	bread		
h	bold		

Narrator

When we read a story, it is the **narrator's** viewpoint we are reading.

Sometimes the narrator is one of the characters in the story.

> He tore my magazine, so I'm taking his precious car. It's as simple as that.

Sometimes the narrator is not in the story at all.

> Cassie was furious with Joe, and paid him back by taking his favourite toy car.

Who the narrator is determines how we see the story.

I In the short section of story below, the narrator is not part of the story. Look at what Cassie and Joe say, and the words they use. Then answer the questions about what you think they might be like.

Joe marched into Cassie's room and grabbed his toy car. 'It's mine!' he shouted, and kicked over the neat pile of books Cassie had just made. 'Get out, brat,' squealed Cassie, throwing her shoe at him.
'I'm telling Mummy,' he yelled back.

But he didn't tell Mum. He just sat on his bed, blinking back tears, and wishing he was old enough to really teach Cassie a lesson.

a How old do you think Joe is? _____

b Is he older, or younger, than Cassie? _____

c How old might Cassie be? _____

d What might the relationship be between Cassie and Joe? _____

e Do you think they often argue like this? _____

II Write the story again twice, first with Joe as the narrator, then Cassie. Try to write it using the kinds of words each character might use if they were telling the story directly to you.

Joe's story:

_____
_____
_____
_____

Cassie's story:

_____
_____
_____
_____

Another spelling rule

Using a spelling rule can help us add suffixes to words ending in a modifying e.

A modifying e changes the vowel sound in the middle of a word, making it a long, drawn-out sound.

hop	hope
short **o** sound	long **oe** sound

If the suffix you want to add starts with a vowel, you must remove the modifying e from the base word first.

make + ing = making

If the suffix starts with a consonant, you keep the e and just add the suffix.

love + ly = lovely

I Add the suffixes in the table to each of these words.

	+ ing	+ ed	+ ful	+ less
a shame	_____	_____	_____	_____
b hope	_____	_____	_____	_____
c care	_____	_____	_____	_____
d use	_____	_____	_____	_____

II Underline the misspelt word in each sentence. Then write the correct spelling.

a My aunt is liveing in Australia. _____
b I have savd enough money for a new bike. _____
c Craig is makeing a model aeroplane. _____
d Dad has takn my brother to watch the football. _____
e Our new puppy is so adoreable. _____
f We chose the niceest Christmas tree. _____
g It's safest to walk on the pavment. _____
h Dawn's singing is more tunful than mine. _____
i I love bakeing cakes. _____
j My baby sister is very livly. _____

ANSWERS

Page 2

I   er: interest, desperate, generally, generous, offering, literature
    en: deafening, widening

II ary: stationary, boundary, voluntary
    ory: factory, category, history
    ery: jewellery, stationery, lottery
    erence: reference, conference, difference

Page 3

I   audi: audible, audience, audition
    trans: transport, transplant, transfer
    re: reply, reconsider, repeat
    prim: prime, primate, primary
    pre: preview, prevent, prehistoric

II a periscope   e include
    b seclude   f microscope
    c transport   g import
    d teleport or   h conclude
       telescope

Page 4

I   a whenever
    b meanwhile
    c moreover
    d whereas or wherever
    e furthermore
    f nonetheless
    g notwithstanding
    h henceforward

II a as well as
    b despite
    c as a result
    d at the same time
    e from now on
    f every time
    g in order that
    h another thing

Page 5

I   a stay   e there
    b listen to   f from where
    c look at   g here
    d truly   h you

II a near   f towards what
    b enemy   place
    c beautiful   g please
    d says   h go away!
    e you or the

Page 6

I   a run   d swim   g sleeps
    b try   e flies   h plays
    c sing   f washes

II a teacher d horses   g trains
    b cats   e brother h shop
    c boy   f girls

Page 7

I   The active verbs are: a, b, e, g, h
    The passive verbs are: c, d, f, i, j

II a The cat chased the mouse.
    b The rain soaked my clothes.
    c Sam found the missing book.
    d Jo opened the door.
    e The paperboy delivered my magazine.
    f The teacher marked our test papers.

Page 8

I   a Who is that, knocking at the door?
    b I felt ill, so I went to bed.
    c We went swimming in the river.
    d It was dark when we got home.
    e We went to Italy for our holiday.
    f I broke the vase when I was dusting.
    g Mum made me a cake for my birthday.
    h The car broke down, because it had run out of petrol.
    i Gran went shopping to buy some slippers.
    j I drew a picture to hang on the wall.

II Many answers are possible.

Page 9

I   a The cat (a tabby) curled up and went to sleep.
    b The packed lunch (a ham sandwich) was delicious.
    c After school (but before tea) we played in the park.
    d The cold rain (and freezing wind) kept us indoors.
    e My little brother's hair (which he cut himself) looks dreadful.
    f The football (kicked by Paul) flew over the fence.

II a My best friend (who is ten) is called Lily.
    b The old dog was dirty (and smelly).
    c Pink (but not pale pink) is my favourite colour. Or,
       Pink is my favourite colour (but not pale pink).
    d My new coat (bought yesterday) is really warm.
    e My new school (where I'm going in September) is really big.
    f The school holiday (which starts next week) is going to be great.

Page 10

I   We sat by the ruined cottage to have our picnic. The sun smiled down on us, and birds chattered in the trees. All around us, buttercups danced in the breeze, and the nodding branches of a willow tree sheltered us from the fierce sun. The broken windows of the deserted cottage stared silently towards the sleeping hills in the distance, and the wind whispered secrets through the empty rooms.

II Many answers are possible.

Page 11

I   Examples of biography are: a, d, f.
    Examples of autobiography are: b, c, e.

II Exact answers may vary.
    When she was eight, she was sent to a strict girls' boarding school. She missed her family terribly and never settled into school life, so she was thrilled when the war came and she was evacuated to Wales with her three brothers. For the next four years they lived on a farm, so it was a dreadful shock for her to return to post-war London, and to school.

Page 12

I   a The grass is always greener on the other side.
    b The early bird catches the worm.
    c A bird in the hand is worth two in the bush.
    d Great minds think alike.
    e Every cloud has a silver lining.
    f A bad workman blames his tools.
    g Many a true word is said in jest.
    h Let sleeping dogs lie.

II Exact wording may vary.
    a A job is easier if shared between many people.
    b Don't risk everything on one go.
    c A problem is easier to solve if two people work together.
    d Mending things sooner saves time in the long run.
    e From one unpleasant situation to another.
    f Never assume things will be as you expect.
    g Think ahead before you take a big decision.

Page 13

I   The adverbs are:
    a silently   f there
    b outside   g slowly
    c quickly   h angrily
    d never   i unsteadily
    e later   j always

II a quickly   e nearly
    b here   f happily
    c brightly   g soundly
    d always   h soon

Page 14

I   a emptiness   f windier
    b frying   g silliness
    c denied   h carrying
    d readily   i friendly
    e sleepily

II a lazily   f happiness
    b hungrily   g heaviest
    c tried   h prettier
    d replied   i terrified
    e married

Page 15

I   a while   e but
    b because   f although
    c so   g before
    d because of   h so

II a because   d before
    b so   e but
    c while   f although or while

Page 16

I   Answers may vary slightly.
    The Vikings invaded Britain more than a thousand years ago. They sailed from Sweden, Norway and Denmark in longboats, and raided the coasts and rivers of the United Kingdom. Many also settled here and farmed the land. Viking families lived in houses made from wood,